A

Supernatural

Metamorphosis

C.E.

A Supernatural Metamorphosis

Copyright © 2022 by C.E.

ISBN 9798420406434

Dedication

Twin Flames

We are different but the same.

When you hurt, I feel your pain.

When I feel less than whole you complete me.

Yin and Yang.

We are different but the same.

When I'm falling apart you keep me sane.

The same soul but different brains.

Twin flames, Yin and Yang.

A bond that words could never explain.

Caterpillar

The Pit of Loneliness 1

Feeling alone, she thought back to the pain she had been successfully ignoring. It was still there, but with no complaints in the present, why would she be so ungrateful? Wanting to cry but having forgotten how, she was comfortably numb. She didn't know why she felt this way; she had come so far. Experiencing complete peace for the first time in her life she didn't want to go without it. She used to sell her body and soul, so she knew what it was like to be completely hopeless and shattered. It was a feeling she would never forget. God was granting her peace and serenity, but she was still not whole. As she studied the missing pieces of her soul, heartache and loneliness crept back in and slowly strangled the joy and peace that had taken her so long to possess. Being naturally drawn to people who didn't need or want her, she began to devalue her worth again. Please God, she begged, remind me what it feels like to love myself.

She was comfortable feeling broken and alone. Loving herself whole was too painful. She broke her newfound peace and worth. She knew it would be painful, but a familiar numbness settled in. How could she deal with success when she had never accomplished anything worthwhile? She gave the most precious parts of herself to ungrateful and undeserving people again. The wound that had almost healed ripped open and out bled violent memories filled with heartache. She couldn't make it stop. She had thought they were shoved away hidden in the darkest corners of her soul, hoping to shed them someday, like a snake sheds its skin. The pain became suffocating. Instead of the skin shedding, she realized the pain was a boa constrictor, wrapping tighter and tighter. Her self-love, her self-worth, and the fire in her soul was smothered until there were only ashes left. She subjected herself to pain and loneliness because she thought it was all that she deserved. She had convinced herself that maybe God's purpose for her life was to please men by selling her body because it brought them pleasure. Her soul withered away, but on the outside she smiled. With life no longer in her eyes or soul, she decided that she couldn't do it anymore. She wanted to rebuild herself somewhere far away from this world, this life. She knew it would bring never-ending sadness to the ones she loved the most. She looked to the sky for motivation, took a deep breath and closed her eyes. "Just hold on, I am here," said God. She knew she could hold on a little longer since it was for the people that she loved and not for herself. She decided not to give into the demons that haunted her dreams. Instead, she forced herself numb again, this time not so comfortably. The pain grew as the peace became more elusive. She was exhausted. She wondered if she could keep going.

A Letter to Myself

I haven't loved you for a long time. I'm sorry I didn't realize your worth and sold you for my own selfish needs and wants. I used you and threw you away like trash. I poured poison into your blood and stomach, had you beaten and raped. I used you like you were nothing. I wish I would have shown you love instead of allowing your boundaries and body to be violated. I taught your mind how to leave your body to survive the things you didn't want to do. I killed your soul and turned you into a shell of who you were meant to be. I lied to you and told you that you weren't worth anything and never would be. I didn't care about your well-being or your beautiful mind. I should have nourished you and watered you like the beautiful flower that you were meant to become. Who knows how much I have held you back just by not believing in you? Please forgive me for not giving you the love you needed.

Winter

     She sacrificed parts of herself to give life to others. When she had given all of herself to people who only knew how to take, she built a wall around the deepest part of her soul. There she stored the love of the universe equaled with an unbearable pain. The wall was built because she had to stay strong to bring God's love to a cold world. The wall became so high that her smile fell into a blank stare and the light in her eyes faded. She was gone to a far place where she could be at peace. She felt no pain, no joy, and no regret. She had transcended the chaos of the world. She knew she couldn't stay long because she was meant to bring light to the world, which meant burning herself.

Detached

I despise my feelings. Anyone or anything that I have ever loved or am falling in love with either leaves or gets taken away. If it doesn't, I push it away. I place distance between people or things that have the potential to make me care about them. Instead of following my heart, I pull away because it brings less pain.

Feeding the Bad Wolf

My mom just called and said she's been having dreams of me again. Waking up, tossing, and turning, praying soon that this will end. If I could fix myself I would have already. I wish I could bring her some relief. I wish I could put her at peace. This demon won't get off me. It takes priceless gifts given to me and trades them for temporary illusions of worldly grief. Empty again although I pretend, I write with my pen contemplating how my life will end. Dying sober or living dead? I struggle with life but try to pretend. I feel like a puzzle with misshapen edges, soaked in vodka and burned from forgotten cigarettes.

My ears are ringing, my face stinging. I pick myself up from the floor and look at you in shock. You were worse than the others because I believed you. You told me God gave men muscles not to oppress women but to protect them. My heart hungry for love ate the insincerity of your lies like it was the last meal it would ever get. Even when my intuition told me to run and get away from you, I pushed the warning to the side. Was I on a suicide mission? Being so bent on self-destruction could it be considered anything different?

What Part of Yourself Would You Give Away?

My destructive self. The one that doesn't have any interest in connecting in authentic relationships with others. The one that puts me through pain and misery because it thinks I am not worthy of happiness and peace. The piece of my soul that holds my most shameful moments and disastrous failures. The piece that says I am not good enough to have love. The stagnant swamp in my soul that is complacent and holds me prisoner in the hole of self-pity and self-hate.

Out of Place

No matter how far I go I am still in the same place. Vodka on my breath, heart taped together with a band-aid. Not stopping now, not stopping now. They say it's not all about what you can see and the things of this world so then why do we all try to fit into the mold. I put the past down. The harder I try the further it seems. Heart bursting open, ripping at the seams. Please take this pain. I can't take it anymore.

They Say You Have to Love Yourself First

A part of my soul is trying to break free from the gates of hell. The one that creeps up and waits for me in the dark alleyways of my being. It's plotting to kill me with its grief, shame, and self-hate. It does not care if I make it to my fullest potential or if I don't fulfill my purpose in this life. It has no emotions or feelings for other souls and has no interest in anything earthly. I have been trying to suffocate it like a fire in my heart. But no, this one is not heavenly, the burn is painful.

Chrysalis

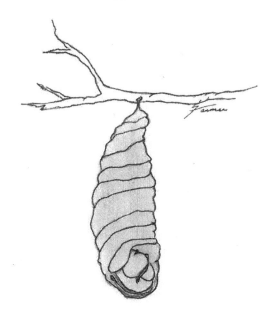

Midnight Thoughts

I smile when I'm dying inside. I don't talk about my feelings for a reason. I have to make myself laugh to see a point in living. I'm tired, exhausted really. Always having to put myself back together. Glue on my hands and tears in my eyes I dust myself off. I hear a voice say to me, "No baby girl, this isn't you. Shake this demon off that tells you that you are nothing. You are the whole ocean in one drop. The eternal universe lives inside of you.

What You Focus on Grows

      I am trying to focus on myself. It sounds selfish but for me it's a task. When my soul is aching and broken, I reach outward rather than inward trying to heal it. To grow I need to keep peeling the layers back. When I believe I have reached my spiritual destination is when I realize I still have a lifetime to go. In the Bible it says to guard your heart, but I built walls around mine lined with armed guards. I have faith that things will get better because I have made it through many hardships by the grace of God.

When You Feel Like Giving Up

God,

    Please help me to keep doing the right things. I want to take back control and go back to doing what I know. I'm trying to be patient and keep doing the next right thing. I just don't know how long I am going to have to feel insecure and uncertain.

Amen.

Another Life Paradox

I had always taken pride in being a strong person. I thought that drifting through the pain, fear and uncertainty of my surroundings was what made me strong. Then God showed me that breaking free from the chains is what makes me a strong person. Facing my feelings instead of numbing and ignoring them.

God,

Please show me how to live. I feel like a lost sheep wandering and looking for your guidance. Please help me choose wisely in this confusing, shiny world. Any light you shine into me please help me give away to others.

Amen.

This Shiny World

One day when all the beautiful souls left in this decrepit world die, the real dream of hell will begin. Many angels still inhabit this planet but, when they are gone there will be no joy, no hope, and no sunlight left. Compared to hell this Earth is a garden. Through pain, through tears, through betrayal and despair, God gives us opportunities to seek Him. He knew before putting us on this planet that He is our only purpose and hope. He watches as we fumble in the dark for the key tied around our neck that will unlock us from the chains of this world. Instead, we find other shiny things to temporarily fulfill our longing. In the darkness everything has a certain glimmer of light. Until we give up and make the ultimate sacrifice, the only definition of true defeat.

Evolving

I was like a dandelion that had managed to grow through the cracked cement. I needed light, love, and water to grow. I was near a sidewalk in front of a house. Sometimes the kind man would come outside and stop to take a closer look at me. I loved it when he did that, it made me feel so special. "You are such a pretty flower. I would love to look at you every day. Maybe when you are strong enough, I will pick you and bring you inside with me." Years went by and with each passing year I would try to come back brighter and more confident that it would be the year he would pick me. One day he stepped on me and didn't even look down. I smashed into the cement and thought surely, I would not come back from this. Next spring came around and I bloomed! I was elated! Only when I grew for myself did I bloom more beautifully than I could have imagined. That is when I learned that I am the strongest when I bloom for myself.

The Unilateral Contract

Most people are not fortunate enough to live one full life. God has blessed me with two. In the first life I played the victim, defeated and alone. Not the kind of alone when you are by yourself. The kind where the room is filled with the people you love most smiling and laughing. You try to because you wish you felt that way, because you wish you felt that way. Instead, you're empty and numb. Not because you don't have a heart but because you gave it to all the wrong people. When I played the victim this world and its people were cold, and I could only trust myself. This world I learned, only wanted to take from me and I had nothing left to give. I was defeated. You in return gave me never-ending love. Like a phoenix rises from the ashes You lifted me to new heights and took my soul out of hell. You turned my weakness into Your strength. You showed me that I had the telescope pointed the wrong way. That everyone is only searching for one thing. Only You can fill my heart with Your love.

Empty Cups

When I am alone, I feel empty. I get my value from others because I see none in myself. I am an empty cup searching for the pitcher when it is only You that can quench the deep need of your love in my heart.

Onions

I am learning to give my worries to God. I see that when I do that everything seems to fall into place. Why is it so uncomfortable? I know that His plans are much bigger and higher than I can imagine. He has given me a new perspective. Every time I think my spiritual work is done; I peel back another layer. I fall apart and rebirth.

It's The Journey

Maybe I am giving myself what I think I deserve. What if instead I chose to forgive myself for the times I failed and made the wrong choices. If I used the infinite amount of energy and wisdom my Creator gave me and nurtured it into self-love. Some days are easier than others and some days I still look past myself in the mirror. "You are beautiful. You are strong." I tell myself as my therapist suggested. Even if I don't believe it yet.

Overcoming You

I still have nightmares that I can't get away from you. I wake up soaked in cold sweat thanking God it's just a dream. I must forgive you, but only for me. It's a half truth because some sick part of me wants to hold onto the anger and disgust. It wants the healed part of me to suffocate at the hands of the same soul who turned me cold. It wants you to be the end of me, but I will not let it.

Heaven on Earth

Instead of collecting things I have started collecting experiences and feelings. Happy and sad, good, and bad. I think that's what we were created for. Can you imagine if the world channeled all its energy into love and compassion instead of greed, money, envy, and fear? In a world where kindness is rarer than coldness it is easy to conform. If you can't see the light, then be it.

Keep Going

I know the feeling. You start wondering if you're even worth the amount of energy it takes for you to keep going. You start doubting yourself because your soul is weak right now. But just know that God is holding you. He knows you're weak and He will never leave you or forsake you. Even though sometimes you feel alone, and the world feels cold. Keep burning, someday you will feel the warmth.

Guardian Angel

Why does God keep sparing me? Maybe, it has nothing to do with me. Maybe it's for another woman I can pull from the gates of hell. Maybe, without me living she would perish too. Maybe, she's you. Maybe she is just beginning her journey through hell. Maybe God is using me to save her because that's what angels do.

Butterfly

A Strong Woman

You didn't think I was that strong, did you? You were sure I would crawl back to you with my tail tucked between my legs. You never understood the fire in my soul. You thought you were powerful enough to put it out. What you didn't know is that a phoenix rises from the ashes, we don't sleep in them.

Rebirth

I know you're tired. I see the struggle in your eyes and feel the ache in your feet. I know you think there's nothing left in you to keep on. What for? Why would peace be so elusive if it was meant for you? Dig deep down into the depths of your soul and find a spark, even if it's just an ember of fading hope. It only has to be the size of a mustard seed. You can do this, not alone, but with God's strength. How many times has it felt like the end, but it bloomed into the most beautiful beginning?

A Message from My Higher Power

You are stronger than you think. I wish you could see yourself through my eyes. You never give up and your faith in Me makes that possible. That is why you keep getting up even on the darkest of days - you see my light guiding you through life's storms. Even though sometimes the waves are so big that you crash down and lose footing, you get up again and move towards My light. No matter how dim it may seem at times. Although sometimes you falter and veer off the path I have for you, I know you will always find your way back home to Me.

Come Alive

I see the light back in your eyes. Even the way your body moves differently when you have hope again. You are a beautiful piece of the Divine. Don't forget, He is closer to you than you are to yourself - the reason you keep on when everything tells you that you can't. Keep your eyes fixed on His light. Give Him all of your weakness, give Him all of you and He will give you His strength.

Lifting Me

She feels hope for the first time in a long time. Buried underneath all her guilt and shame, her feelings of worthlessness and despair. She chose to fan the last hint of burning ember left in her soul. From the depths of despair, she was lifted by the grace of the Divine.

My Sculptor

Take me, I don't want me. Mold me into who you would have me be. Guide me, take my hand and I will follow You. You are the only one who can make me new. I am the sculpture, and You are the Sculptor. Your plans take my pain and turn it into gain. Dying a little every day, You make beauty from my pain. Sometimes the carving of my spirit is painful, but You are within me. Closer than I think You to be. I feel Your grace washing over me, and don't feel the weight of this world so heavily. You set my soul free.

Made in the USA
Middletown, DE
08 April 2023

28299569R00022